Discovering More Science Secrets

by Sandra Markle
Illustrated by June Otani

SCHOLASTIC INC.

New York   Toronto   London   Auckland   Sydney

D0096409

For Shawn Jordan,
whose curiosity and desire to investigate
is an inspiration.

ISBN 0-590-44879-X

Text copyright © 1992 by Sandra Markle.
Illustrations copyright © 1992 by Scholastic Inc.
All rights reserved.   Published by Scholastic Inc.

12 11 10 9 8 7 6 5 4 3 2 1   2 3 4 5 6 7/9

Printed in the U.S.A.   28

First Scholastic printing, April, 1992

Contents

Can you change white glue into rubbery stuff?

Can you find out what colors are hidden in black ink?

Can you use liquid soap to power a toy boat?

Yes, you can do all this and more! All you need are some materials you will find at home or can purchase cheaply at a grocery or hobby store. Then perform the activities in this book to find out how science can help you do some exciting things.

There are some quick quizzes to challenge you, too. They'll let you discover some amazing facts about animals and the weather.

Remember

- Do not do any activity involving a hot stove without an adult to help you.

- Clean up the work area after you finish your project.

- Have fun!

Give Pepper Extra Pep!

Sometimes science can almost seem magical. And here's a little science magic for you to perform.

You'll need:

A pie plate
Water
A shaker containing ground pepper
A cotton-tipped swab
¼ teaspoon of liquid dishwashing soap
Baby powder

Fill the pie plate full of water and wait until the surface appears smooth.

Sprinkle on the pepper until most of the surface is covered.

Dip the cotton-tipped end of the swab into the liquid soap.

Now watch closely because the action happens fast: Touch the soapy tip of the swab to the water in the very center of the pie plate.

Did you see the pepper flakes leap toward the side of the pie plate? To repeat this action, you'll need to rinse out the pie plate, dry it, and then start over.

Why does this happen? Water, like all matter, is made up of tiny building blocks called molecules. The molecules at the surface of the water are strongly attracted to each other and to those molecules below them. This bonding tends to pull the molecules at the surface down and together so that the surface of the water acts as if it has a thin skin.

Scientists refer to this condition as surface tension. Soap lessens the natural attraction between the surface molecules so it "breaks" the skin-like layer. The effect quickly spreads outward toward the edges of the container, and the pepper flakes are carried along. Try this activity using baby powder and you'll see the same results.

Set Colors in Motion

Water isn't the only liquid whose molecules attract each other, creating surface tension. Milk has surface tension, too. This activity will show you how surface tension can make a dazzling color display.

You'll need:

A pie plate
Whole milk
Red, green, yellow, and blue food coloring
Clear or white liquid dishwashing soap

Fill the pie plate nearly full of milk. Sprinkle on about five drops of each of the food colorings.

Pour liquid soap around the entire rim of the pie plate and watch what happens. How long is it before the reaction starts? How long does the colorful explosion continue?

Just as with the leaping pepper flakes, this swirling reaction occurs when the milk's surface tension is disrupted by the soap.

Power-up a Soap Boat

You've already discovered that soap lessens the natural bonding between water molecules. And you've learned that adding soap destroys the skin-like surface tension on a container of water or milk. Now you can use this knowledge to have some fun.

You'll need:

A 2-inch square of heavy-duty aluminum foil (or wash and recycle the foil top from a snack, such as yogurt)
Sharp scissors (Handle with care!)
A 13- by 9-inch rectangular cake pan (or similar-size pan)
Water
Liquid dishwashing soap
A small plate or square of scrap paper
Toothpick

To make your foil boat, first cut a triangle out of the foil. At the very center of the triangle's base, snip out a small, V-shaped wedge. Smooth out the foil with your thumbnail to make it as flat as possible.

Next, fill the cake pan at least half full of water. Set it on the counter and wait until the water is still. Pour a puddle of liquid soap about the size of a quarter on the plate or paper scrap.

Now you're ready for action. So set your boat afloat at one end of the pan and aim its pointed nose toward the opposite end. Dip the tip of a toothpick into the soap puddle and carefully place one drop in the V-shaped wedge at the back of the boat.

Because the soap lessens the natural bonding between the water molecules, the surface tension is broken up at the back of the boat. As you already discovered in "Give Pepper Extra Pep!", this effect quickly spreads toward the edges of the container. The boat, like the pepper flakes, is carried along as this happens.

Remember, each time you want to make the boat go, you'll need to rinse out the pan to get rid of any trace of soap and refill it.

Snake Secrets

Many people think that snakes are slimy, but they're not. While a snake's scaly skin is dry, it is likely to feel cool to the touch. Snakes are cold-blooded, which means that they must depend on their environment to keep their body a temperature at which they can survive.

Want to know some more facts about snakes? Then take this quiz.

1. Since a snake lacks legs, it can't climb trees. True or false?

2. All snakes are deaf. True or false?

3. You can tell a rattlesnake's age by the number of rattles on its tail. True or false?

4. A snake can swallow food much larger than its own head. True or false?

5. A snake's eyes have tears. True or false?

1. *Since a snake lacks legs, it can't climb trees. True or false? False.* Many snakes are good climbers. Snakes have strong muscles. They also have wide, flat, overlapping belly scales, which have sharp edges. These edges catch on rough bits of earth or tree bark, providing traction.

The real secret of a snake's ability to slither and even climb, though, is its many ribs and spinal vertebrae or backbones. It has as many as four hundred. These bones make the snake's long body flexible enough to shift from side to side in a wavy motion, or pull together and push apart like an accordian. And when the muscles that are attached to the ribs lift the belly scales and force them against the ground or tree bark, the snake pushes itself along.

2. *All snakes are deaf. True or false? True.* They can sense vibrations, but they hunt the small animals they eat mostly by scent. They have nostrils that provide a pretty good sense of smell. A snake also "tastes" scents by collecting particles on its forked tongue and flicking the two tips into a special organ in the roof of its mouth.

Some snakes, called pit vipers, also have a sense organ in a pit between their eye and nostril on each side of their head. This special sense organ lets the snake detect heat from warm-blooded animals. So pit vipers can hunt even on the darkest night or underground in a burrow.

3. *You can tell a rattlesnake's age by the number of rattles on its tail. True or false? False.* A rattler's tail is formed by hard bony pieces of unshed skin, and another rattle is added every time the snake molts or sheds its skin to grow bigger. Since rattlers, like all snakes, may molt four times a year when they're young, one rattle doesn't equal one year's growth. After about eight rattles have accumulated, the rattles tend to snap off, too.

Whether the tail is long or short, its rattles make a loud noise when the snake rapidly shakes its tail, and this warning is usually enough to keep a bigger animal from stepping on the snake.

4. *A snake can swallow food much larger than its own head. True or false? True.* This is possible because a snake's lower jaw can stretch open extremely wide. At the front, tissue connects the two halves of the lower jawbone, which also helps the snake to open its mouth wide. Sharp, back-slanting teeth guide food down the throat as large quantities of slippery saliva are produced to keep it sliding. Then very stretchy, flexible skin, plus ribs that are attached only to the backbone, allow the snake's body to stretch to fit its food.

Since swallowing something huge can take as long as an hour, a snake has one final adaptation for taking a *big* bite. It can push its windpipe out the bottom of its mouth so it can keep on breathing even while its mouth is full. Once inside, the food is slowly dissolved by the snake's digestive juices as the muscles move the bulging lump toward the tail end. There, what can't be digested is passed out as waste. After eating such a big meal, snakes often go two weeks or longer before eating again.

5. *A snake's eyes have tears. True or false? True.* It has tears to help lubricate the eyes so they can move freely up and down and back and forth. Instead of being protected by eyelids, a snake's eyes are covered by clear protective scales, kind of like a diver's mask. So the tears never flow outside the eye. Instead, they drain into small cavities inside the snake's head.

Magic Bottle

If you poke a hole in a bottle full of water, will it leak? Not if you know an important science secret. Try this activity to discover that secret for yourself.

You'll need:

An empty 1- or 2-liter plastic soft drink bottle with a screw-on cap
Water
2 pushpins (pins with large heads used to display things on bulletin boards)

Work outdoors or at the sink. Fill the bottle to the very top with water. Screw the cap on, making sure it's tightly sealed.

Next, stick one pushpin into the soft side of the bottle above the hard plastic base. Push the second pushpin into the opposite side of the bottle. Then pull out both pins. Surprise! If water leaks out at all, it quickly stops.

Did the bottle magically plug itself? Of course not. Place your hands on the bottle and squeeze. You'll see water spurt out both holes. But when you stop squeezing, the water will immediately stop flowing.

What's happening?

The science secret that makes this bottle appear to magically "plug" its own holes is air pressure. Even though it's invisible, air has weight and takes up space. Air doesn't simply push down, though. It exerts force in all directions. And the force of the air pushing in on the water at the holes you made is greater than that of the water inside the bottle pushing out.

What do you think would happen if you took the cap off the bottle, letting air push down on the water inside the bottle? Try it and find out.

The Truth About Elephants — Maybe

You probably already know that elephants are the biggest living land animals. But did you know that, just like people, elephants tend to be right- or left-handed? In the elephant's case, it's one tusk or the other that gets favored. Or did you know that an elephant sometimes piles branches on its head to act as a sun shade?

Besides taking care of themselves, elephants help each other. If one elephant is hurt, the other members of its herd provide protection until it recovers. And several female elephants are always on hand to baby-sit when a mother needs to leave her youngster long enough to enjoy a cool swim.

Want to know more fascinating facts about elephants? Then don't miss this quiz.

1. An elephant's trunk is used only to pick up food. True or false?

2. An elephant is annoyed by the birds that often land on its back. True or false?

3. An elephant can walk very fast, but it can't jump even an inch. True or false?

4. An elephant has only four teeth with which to chew its food. True or false?

5. An elephant's skin is about an inch thick. True or false?

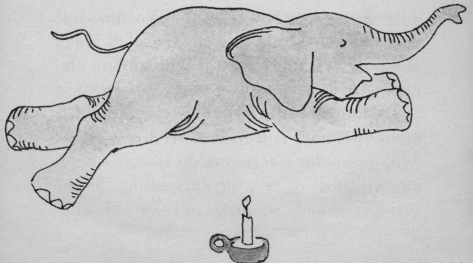

1. *An elephant's trunk is used only to pick up food. True or false? False.* A full-grown elephant's trunk is a 6-foot long, 300-pound, muscular tool that is perfect for picking up food, but it can also do a lot more. To get a drink, an elephant sucks up about a gallon of water in its trunk and squirts it into its mouth.

Elephants greet each other by poking the tips of their trunks into each other's mouths. A mother uses her trunk to hug or caress her calf. She also gives her youngster a trunk spanking if it's unruly. When traveling, elephants often keep track of each other by wrapping their trunk around the tail of the elephant just ahead.

An elephant also uses its trunk to smell in all directions and to breathe when swimming or walking across deep rivers. And if an elephant is angry, the earsplitting "trumpeting" sound is produced by blowing through its trunk.

2. *An elephant is annoyed by the birds that often land on its back. True or false?* *False.* These birds are welcomed because they eat the insects that irritate the elephant's sensitive skin. They also fly away when they spot danger, which warns the elephants that trouble is nearby.

3. *An elephant can walk very fast, but it can't jump even an inch. True or false?* *True.* Elephants normally average 4 to 5 miles per hour, but they can walk as fast as 20 miles per hour. They can't jump even an inch, though, because the impact of just a small bounce would be enough to cause their great weight to crush their legs upon landing.

4. *An elephant has only four teeth with which to chew its food. True or false? True.* An elephant has only one tooth in each half of its upper and lower jaw. Each of these teeth, though, is as big as a soccer ball and weighs about 9 pounds. An elephant needs big teeth because it needs to chew or crush a lot of vegetation. A big male elephant may eat as much as 600 pounds of food every day.

All this chewing wears down the elephant's teeth. Luckily, when one set of teeth wears out, the whole set falls out and is replaced by another set. The new set of teeth is made out of even more layers of hard enamel cemented together to make it durable. An elephant's first set of teeth has only three layers of enamel, while its last set has nine layers.

An elephant's teeth can be replaced six times if it lives a full life. When the last set of teeth is lost, the elephant starves to death because it's unable to chew its food. Luckily, each set of teeth lasts a long time because elephants may live to be more than 60 years old.

5. *An elephant's skin is about an inch thick. True or false? True.* While an elephant's skin is thick, it isn't an armor coat. In fact, it's extremely sensitive.

An elephant bathes at least once a day to keep its skin soft and clean. As soon as it emerges from the water, though, the elephant rolls in dust. This becomes mud on the elephant's wet body and when the mud dries, it becomes a protective coating that shields the elephant's skin from biting insects. When the mud cracks and becomes itchy, the elephant takes another bath. The elephant's color usually depends on the color of the dirt covering its skin.

Build a Stack of Liquids

All liquids mix together when you pour one into the other. True or false?

If you've ever poured vegetable oil into a glass of water, you know the answer is false. The reason is that while everything is made up of molecules, these tiny building blocks don't always have the same amount of space between them. It's easy to understand that the molecules in a solid piece of steel are more tightly packed together than the molecules are in water. Some liquids, though, have molecules more tightly packed than those in water. And some liquids have their molecules less tightly packed than those in water.

The spacing of a material's molecules determines that material's density, or thickness. And you can use the densities of different liquids to make them stack up. Then you can use this liquid stack to compare the densities of some solids. First, follow the steps to build the density stack, and then perform the test.

You'll need:

A tall, skinny, clear glass or plastic container, such as an empty olive jar

¼ cup clear corn syrup

¼ cup water with three drops of red food coloring added

¼ cup vegetable oil

¼ cup rubbing alcohol with three drops of yellow food coloring added

Sharp scissors (Handle with care!)

The white of a hard-boiled egg

A Styrofoam packing peanut or a piece of a Styrofoam cup

A pebble about the size of the tip of your little finger

Be sure the container is clean and dry. Pour in the corn syrup, allowing time for it to completely settle in the bottom of the container.

Slowly add the colored water, tilting the container and letting the liquid slip gently down the side. Next, add the vegetable oil in the same way. And finally, pour in the colored rubbing alcohol.

When all the liquids have been added and allowed to settle, look through the side of the container. You'll see that the liquids are separated in distinct layers with the densest — the corn syrup — on the bottom, and the least dense — the rubbing alcohol — on the top. Next, carefully cut out a piece of egg white and a chunk of the Styrofoam packing peanut or cup about the same size as the pebble.

Drop the piece of egg white into the liquid stack and wait until it stops dropping. It will come to rest when it is lighter than the liquid below it. If it is heavier than all the liquids, it will sink to the very bottom of the container. Where does the egg white stop?

Now test the Styrofoam piece and the pebble in the same way. How does the density of each of these compare to the egg white? To the liquids in the stack?

Find samples of other materials to test. For example, you might want to try a plastic bead, a piece of hot dog, a piece of carrot, or a piece of wood.

Find Out What Colors Are Hidden in Black Ink

Black ink looks black, but it's really a mixture of different colored inks. You can use the different densities of the inks to separate them. Then you can see this secret color mix for yourself.

You'll need:

A medium- to large-sized coffee filter
Scissors (Handle with care!)
A ruler
A plastic straw or a pencil
A small glass (such as a juice glass)
A black watercolor marking pen
Water

First you will have to cut a strip of the coffee filter that will be hung inside the glass.

Cut the strip from the center of the filter. Make it two inches wide and about one inch longer than the height of your glass.

Now fold the top of the strip down about an inch.

Cut two slits about ½ inch apart.

Unfold the strip and slip the straw or pencil through both slits.

Now lay the straw or pencil across the top of the glass. The filter strip should just

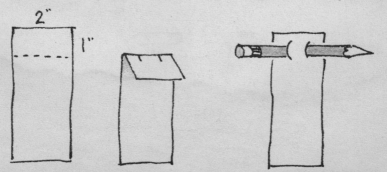

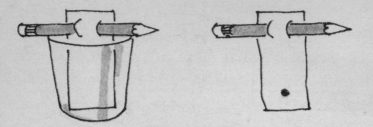

touch the bottom. If it is too long, trim it. (Don't worry if it is a little too short.)

Next, lift the strip out and make a spot of ink on it about one inch from the bottom. The ink spot should be about as big as the tip of your little finger.

Pour a little water into the glass to the depth of about a quarter of an inch.

Lower the paper strip into the water as you lay the straw across the top of the glass again.

Watch as the water rises up through the filter paper. What color appears first? How many different colors do you see?

You were able to discover the different colors that combined to produce the black ink because each had a slightly different density. So each was carried upward by the water at a different rate. The least dense material travels the fastest and is at the top of the colorful display. The next-least dense material travels a little slower and appears a little farther down, and so forth.

This process, called chromatography, is used by scientists to discover the ingredients of a substance. It's also used by police investigators to discover, for example, if a check or document has been altered. Ink samples from the part thought to be real and the part thought to be forged are analyzed using this separation process.

Even different batches of the same brand of ink have slightly different compositions, so the colorful pattern produced by the ink will be the same only if the inks are identical.

Going Ape

Gorillas, chimpanzees, orangutans, and gibbons are all members of the ape family. Gorillas, the biggest members of this group, are sometimes shown as giants in movies. Even though they're never that large, male gorillas do get to be as tall as 5 feet 8 inches, and weigh about 450 pounds.

Also in the movies, chimpanzees often give a toothy smile. People who have studied chimp behavior have learned that chimps show their teeth as a threat. They express friendliness by pulling back their lips at the corners while masking their teeth.

Want to know some more facts about apes? Then take this quiz.

1. Gorillas build nests. True or false?

2. Gorillas are fierce, violent animals. True or false?

3. All apes are good at swinging through the trees. True or false?

4. Chimpanzees use tools and weapons. True or false?

5. All apes live in large, communal groups. True or false?

1. *Gorillas build nests. True or false? True.* When it starts to get dark, a gorilla selects its sleeping spot and then constructs a nest. Usually about five feet across, the center of the nest is left bare, and leafy branches are piled up around the sides. If there are large enough trees around, the gorilla builds its nest in the tree's branches. Although a new nest is built each evening, the gorilla works fast. On the average, gorillas take about two minutes to construct a nest on the ground, and five to ten minutes to build one in a tree.

2. *Gorillas are fierce, violent animals. True or false? False.* Although they are the largest and heaviest apes, gorillas are peaceful. If confronted by danger, they generally try to slip away into the brush. However, to protect its group, a male gorilla may stand up, beat its chest, roar loudly, and show its teeth.

3. *All apes are good at swinging through the trees. True or false? False.* Gibbons are the best, being able to attain speeds up to

40 miles per hour. They can also launch themselves across gaps spanning as much as 30 feet.

Chimps are also pretty good at this branch-to-branch maneuver. Adult gorillas are too heavy for all but the strongest trees, so they mainly walk on the ground. Adult orangutans manage to move from limb to limb, but only slowly and awkwardly, using both their arms and legs. Even being careful, though, these big adult apes frequently fall. Young orangutans and gorillas are good swingers.

4. *Chimpanzees use tools and weapons. True or false? True.* Chimpanzees have been observed poking sticks and branches into termite holes and then eating the termites they collect. Some chimps also have been observed chewing leaves and then plunging these spongy wads into holes in trees to soak up the water trapped inside. They've also been observed throwing sticks and stones at enemies.

5. *All apes live in large, communal groups. True or false? False.* Orangutans usually live alone. Chimpanzees are very social animals, though, and often live with as many as 80 other chimps in a group.

One reason the chimp groups become so large is that the young stay with their mother for about six years. And females like to remain in contact with their mother, even after they have young of their own.

The size of gorilla groups varies greatly from as few as five to as many as 40. These groups are always under the direction of one male leader. He not only provides protection, he also indicates to the group when to rest and when to be active, where to look for food, and where to travel. He also disciplines any unruly youngsters by giving them a harsh glare.

Gibbons are unique among apes, living in just single family groups with a mother, a father, and up to three youngsters of different ages.

Create a Crystal Garden

You can use some household items and chemicals to create a fanciful display. Then you can water it to watch it grow again and again.

You'll need:

3 clean, dry sponges
A 9-inch aluminum pie pan
A measuring cup
$\frac{1}{4}$ cup table salt
$\frac{1}{4}$ cup water
$\frac{1}{4}$ cup laundry bluing (available at grocery stores in the laundry soap area) or liquid Bluette (follow the directions on the bottle to make a bluing solution)
1 tablespoon household ammonia
A mixing bowl
A metal spoon
Food coloring

Arrange the sponges any way you wish in the middle of the pie pan. The sponges can overlap.

Pour the salt, water, bluing, and ammonia into the bowl and stir to mix well. Then pour the liquid over the sponges, and spoon on the remaining thick portion, spreading it out. Finally, sprinkle on drops of each of the food colors.

Let the pan sit. As the liquid begins to evaporate or move into the air, crystals develop. Depending upon the temperature and air circulation, this may take only hours, or it may take several days for crystals to first appear.

The change from liquid to crystals takes place because the molecules of salt that dissolve or become suspended in the solution collect around the tiny particles of bluing. Then as the liquid evaporates, the molecules begin to arrange themselves in patterns. The pattern of a salt crystal is a cube, but the faster the crystals form, the tinier they are.

The ammonia helps speed up the evaporation process so the crystals that form are tiny and so close together that they bump into each other. Like a pile of cube-shaped building blocks heaped together, the overall view of the crystals is irregular.

When all of the liquid has evaporated, no new crystals will form. So sprinkle on enough water to return the chemicals to a solution, and you'll be able to watch the crystals develop all over again.

Does temperature affect how quickly crystals first appear? Try placing the container in a location that is cool and then repeat the experiment, placing the container in a warm spot.

Make Silver Shine
Without Touching It

Something made out of silver, such as jewelry or tableware, loses its luster and turns dark if left out in the air. When this happens, the metal is said to be tarnished. The shine can be returned by rubbing the silver with a polish. Or you can do it almost as if by magic, by using chemistry. Just ask an adult to work with you and follow the steps on the next two pages.

You'll need:

1 to 5 pieces of tarnished silver
A sheet of heavy-duty aluminum foil about
a foot long
1 teaspoon baking soda
1 teaspoon salt
A large metal saucepan or a frying pan
Water

Place the tarnished pieces of silver side by side on the shiny side of the aluminum foil. Sprinkle on the baking soda and salt.

Fold the free ends of the foil over the silver, rolling the edges together to seal. Press the foil packet to be sure all parts of the tarnished articles are in contact with the aluminum.

Put the foil packet in the pan. Cover with water.

Boil for five minutes. Carefully remove the pan from the heat and let the water completely cool.

Remove the packet and take out the silver. Rinse and dry.

Were you surprised with the results? If any spots of tarnish remain, you can be sure those places weren't in contact with the aluminum foil. You could repeat the process, taking special care to press the foil against any remaining dark spots.

The silver became tarnished when its surface molecules reacted with the sulfur that naturally occurs in the air. In this chemical reaction, the aluminum reacts with the tarnish, and the silver is restored to its metallic gleam.

Weather Wonders

The weather usually determines the way you dress and often affects what you do. It's a very important part of the world around you, and sometimes it can be absolutely amazing. For example, in just 24 hours in 1952, Cilaos on Réunion Island in the Indian Ocean received 74 inches of rain. And nearly 600 flashes of lightning occur somewhere in the world every second. Java, in fact, has lightning 300 days a year.

Want to check out more fascinating weather facts? Then this quiz is for you.

1. Hailstones can sometimes be as big as softballs, or even bigger. True or false?

2. Lightning bolts travel only from the clouds to the ground. True or false?

3. Tornadoes, the fiercest storms on Earth, are huge, cutting a path of damage hundreds of miles wide. True or false?

4. The center of a hurricane has the strongest winds. True or false?

5. One record snowfall dumped 100 feet of snow on a town in Colorado in 24 hours. True or false?

1. *Hailstones can sometimes be as big as softballs, or even bigger. True or false?* *True.* While most hailstones are no larger than the size of a pea, some get to be quite large. The biggest ever discovered was the size of a melon and weighed 1.67 pounds. It landed in Coffeyville, Kansas, on September 3, 1970. Hailstones form when wind tosses an ice particle back up inside a cloud each time it starts to drop. As it falls, water

droplets collect on the particle and then these are frozen as the hailstone soars upward. In this way, layers of ice build up, one on top of the other, and the hailstone grows bigger and bigger.

2. *Lightning bolts travel only from the clouds to the ground. True or false?* *False.* While it may appear that lightning is streaking downward from the clouds, the energy is actually going in both directions. First, a very thin "pilot leader" streaks down from the cloud. Just before it reaches the ground, though, the brilliant flash that we call lightning leaps upward from the ground and follows the path of the leader to the cloud. This surge of charged particles travels at the speed of light (186,000 miles per second). It's also extremely hot, heating the air around it up to 50,000° F. This super-hot air expands very quickly, and the cooler air rushing in to replace it creates the boom we recognize as thunder.

3. *Tornadoes, the fiercest storms on Earth, are huge, cutting a path of damage hundreds of miles wide. True or false? False.* Tornadoes are the world's fiercest storms, but luckily even the largest has been estimated to be only about 1,600 feet across. The winds of these storms, though, reach speeds of more than 200 miles per hour. So wherever a tornado touches down, it destroys everything in its path. These winds are so powerful that they've been known to embed straw into wooden telephone poles, uproot trees, and lift a heavy locomotive off its tracks.

If a tornado warning is issued for your area, this means that a tornado has been spotted. You should immediately take action to protect yourself. The safest place to be is in the basement under the stairs, or under a heavy piece of furniture.

4. *The center of a hurricane has the strongest winds. True or false? False.* Hurricanes, or typhoons as they're called in the China Seas, are very large and fierce storms. Winds may reach 190 miles per hour, and the storm cloud may extend over many miles. There's likely to be a short-lived break in the storm, though, when the center or "eye" passes over an area. Hurricanes are cycling storms, and in the very center there is a very calm region where the air doesn't rise. Immediately encircling the eye, though, are the worst winds and rain of the entire storm.

5. *One record snowfall dumped 100 feet of snow on a town in Colorado in 24 hours. True or false? False.* The town of Silver Lake, Colorado, does hold the real record, though. This community received 76 inches of snow in 24 hours from April 14 to April 15 in 1921.

The deepest snows in the United States fall in the mountains of California, Oregon, and Washington. This is because winds carry moisture from the ocean up the mountains where snows form and are dumped. Canada and New England also get a lot of snow.

The North and South Poles, which are noted for being covered with huge glaciers, actually receive surprisingly little new snow each year. But since it's so cold at the poles, most of the snow that falls never melts, and what is there has accumulated over hundreds of years.

Make Some Glue Putty

You probably think of white glue as a sticky liquid that can be used to hold things together. It is that, of course, but it is also the basic ingredient for a whole new kind of material. Follow the steps below to make "glue putty." Then perform the tests to see how this material differs from the original glue.

You'll need:

A plastic garbage bag
3 tablespoons Faultless powdered starch (scented, gloss, or any other brand of starch will not work)

¼ cup water

A large plastic or paper cup

A tablespoon

A measuring cup

¼ cup white glue (Elmer's Glue-All or Elmer's School Glue works best)

A self-sealing plastic bag to store the putty

Cover your work area with the garbage bag.

Mix three tablespoons of starch and ¼ cup of water in the large cup, stirring well with the spoon.

Pour the glue into the cup. Press it and mix it with the spoon for about a minute until a thick material forms.

Now you have to rinse it off. Take the cup to the sink. Run a small amount of water into the cup, swirl it around, and pour the water out.

Press the mixture in the cup with the spoon again.

Then rinse it once more, holding the cup under the running water while you count very slowly to ten.

Remove the glue putty from the cup. Hold it over the sink to let any remaining liquid drain off the putty. Now perform the following tests.

1. Shape it into a ball. Does the ball bounce?
2. What happens when you let the ball sit? Does the ball hold its shape?
3. Try pulling some of the glue putty slowly between your two hands. Does it stretch? Let go and see if it will snap back.
4. What happens when you pull it hard and fast?

All matter is made up of tiny building blocks called molecules. Scientists call molecules *monomers* when they are single units.

When the molecules for a material are linked together into long chains, though, scientists call them *polymers* because they're made up of many monomers. What characteristics the polymer will have depends on what chemicals make up the chain and how they are arranged in the chain. Sometimes groups of chains may even become linked together.

The glue putty you mixed up is a polymer. Now go on to the next section and make another polymer, glubber. Then compare how these two polymers are alike and how they are different.

Make Some Glubber

Start with white glue again, but this time mix it with a solution of Borax and water. Then test this material, comparing it to the glue you started with and to the glue putty you made before.

You'll need:

A plastic garbage bag
A paper cup
A measuring cup
$\frac{1}{4}$ cup water
1 tablespoon Borax (laundry freshener available at grocery stores)
A spoon
$\frac{1}{4}$ cup white glue (Elmer's Glue-All or Elmer's School Glue works best)
A self-sealing plastic bag

Cover your work area with the garbage bag and set the paper cup on it.

Pour the water into the cup. Add the Borax and stir well. Most of the crystals

will dissolve, but some will settle to the bottom.

Pour the white glue into the self-sealing plastic bag. Pour in the liquid from the cup, leaving the remaining crystals in the cup.

Seal the bag and squeeze gently to mix. The glue will soon appear to form a solid lump. Keep squeezing for about a minute after this happens, though. The outer surface may change first, trapping some liquid glue inside. Squeezing frees this glue to mix with the Borax solution.

When you're finished mixing, open the bag, hold it in the sink, and let tap water run into the bag while you count very slowly to ten. Then remove the rinsed glubber and hold it over the sink to let any remaining liquid drain off. Now perform the following tests.

1. Shape it into a ball. Does the ball bounce?
2. What happens when you let the ball sit? Does the ball hold its shape?
3. Try pulling some of the glubber slowly between your two hands. Does it stretch? Let go and see if it will snap back.
4. What happens when you pull it hard and fast?

In what ways is the glubber like the glue putty you made? How is it different?

Even though they each had their own unique characteristics, did both glubber and glue putty remind you a little of a liquid and a little of a solid? These two materials belong to a group of fluids that are interesting because they're a little like both.

Flutter Facts

You've undoubtedly seen butterflies in flight. But did you know that male butterflies often identify females of their own species by their flight patterns?

Want to find out more about butterflies? Then don't miss this quiz.

1. Some butterflies are bigger than some small birds. True or false?

2. Some types of butterflies migrate, flying great distances to spend the winter where it's warmer. True or false?

3. Butterflies have scaly wings. True or false?

4. Butterflies have tiny teeth with which to chew their food. True or false?

5. Some butterflies are brightly colored to protect themselves from predators. True or false?

1. *Some butterflies are bigger than small birds. True or false? True.* The Queen Alexandra's Birdwing, which can be found in the South Pacific, often has a wingspan as big as 11 inches from wingtip to wingtip. Persistent collectors and the destruction of its forest habitat have threatened this butterfly giant.

While you aren't likely to find any butterflies that big in the United States, big swallowtails may have wings that are as much as five inches across. The caterpillars of these butterflies are also big, and in the South, where they feed on citrus trees, they can cause serious crop damage.

2. *Some types of butterflies migrate, flying great distances to spend the winter where it's warmer. True or false? True.* The monarch butterflies fly to Florida, southern California, and Mexico to spend the winter. They travel in groups — sometimes more than 1,000 may travel together. Some fly as far as 4,000 miles.

Once they arrive, they cling to the branches of the trees, hibernating. In the spring, the adults head north again, but they soon lay their eggs and die. The young monarchs that develop from these eggs continue heading north until they spread into Canada.

3. *Butterflies have scaly wings. True or false? True.* A butterfly's wings are covered with thousands of scales that overlap like shingles on a roof. The scales are what give color to the wings. Each scale is attached at one end to a shallow pit in the wing membrane. Because the other end of the scale is loose, they easily fall off, looking like colorful dust on your finger if you touch a butterfly's wing.

The scales also come in many different shapes — round, nearly square, and with scalloped edges. Some are even long and hairlike. These scales cover the butterfly's body and are what give it a hairy appearance.

4. *Butterflies have tiny teeth with which to chew their food. True or false? False.* Butterflies eat by sucking nectar from flowers through a long, coiled tongue or proboscis. The way the butterfly eats is similar to drinking through a straw.

The proboscis is located just under the head and is held coiled up when the butterfly isn't eating. When the butterfly finds a flower and is ready to eat, it extends the proboscis as much as several inches. This makes it possible for the butterfly to eat without actually landing on the flower.

5. *Some butterflies are brightly colored to protect themselves from predators. True or false? True.* Some butterflies are brightly colored to announce that they taste bad or that they're poisonous. Other types of butterflies are colored to mimic these butterflies so that predators will leave them alone, too.